Ff

Bela Davis

abdopublishing.com

Published by Abdo Kids, a division of ABDO, PO Box 398166, Minneapolis, Minnesota 55439.
Copyright © 2017 by Abdo Consulting Group, Inc. International copyrights reserved in all countries.
No part of this book may be reproduced in any form without written permission from the publisher.

Printed in the United States of America, North Mankato, Minnesota.

102016
012017

 THIS BOOK CONTAINS
RECYCLED MATERIALS

Photo Credits: iStock, Shutterstock

Production Contributors: Teddy Borth, Jennie Forsberg, Grace Hansen

Design Contributors: Christina Doffing, Candice Keimig, Dorothy Toth

Publisher's Cataloging in Publication Data

Names: Davis, Bela, author.

Title: Ff / by Bela Davis.

Description: Minneapolis, Minnesota : Abdo Kids, 2017 | Series: The alphabet |
    Includes bibliographical references and index.

Identifiers: LCCN 2016943886 | ISBN 9781680808827 (lib. bdg.) |
    ISBN 9781680795929 (ebook) | ISBN 9781680796599 (Read-to-me ebook)

Subjects: LCSH: English language--Alphabet--Juvenile literature. | Alphabet
    books--Juvenile literature.

Classification: DDC 421/.1--dc23

LC record available at http://lccn.loc.gov/2016943886

Table of Contents

Ff

Four **f**riends have **f**un.

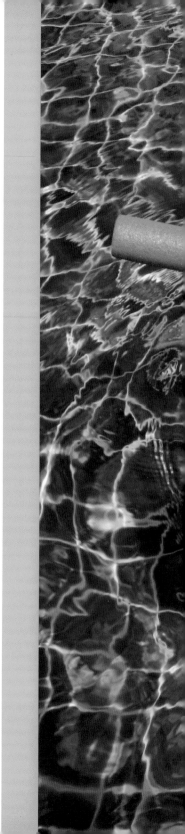

Ff

Fiona sits with her **f**amily.

Ff

Frank wears a **f**ire helmet.

Ff

Fara **f**eeds a **foal** in a **f**ield.

Ff

Freya has **fancy f**lowers.

Ff

Finn **f**lies a plane.

15

Ff

Finley waves a flag.

Ff

Faith eats **fr**esh **fr**uit.

Ff

What is **F**elix behind?

(a **f**ence)

20

More **Ff** Words

farm

feet

feather

football

Glossary

fancy
not plain or ordinary.

foal
a baby horse.

fresh
newly picked and not preserved.

Index

abdokids.com

Use this code to log on to abdokids.com and access crafts, games, videos, and more!

Abdo Kids Code:
TFK8827